SHRINK YOURSELF

THE
COMPLETE DO-IT-YOURSELF GUIDE
TO
FREUDIAN PSYCHOANALYSIS

SHRINK YOURSELF

THE
COMPLETE DO-IT-YOURSELF GUIDE
TO
FREUDIAN PSYCHOANALYSIS

TED MEYER

THOMAS DUNNE BOOKS
St. Martin's Griffin ✠ New York

THOMAS DUNNE BOOKS.
An imprint of St. Martin's Press.

SHRINK YOURSELF:
THE COMPLETE DO-IT-YOURSELF GUIDE TO FREUDIAN PSYCHOANALYSIS

For information, address:
St. Martin's Press, 175 Fifth Avenue, New York, NY 10010

www.stmartins.com

Book design by Future Studio & Art Your World

ISBN 0-312-27222-7

First Edition: February 2001

10 9 8 7 6 5 4 3 2 1

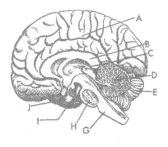

INTRODUCTION

There is an old joke that goes like this: I was having dinner with my mother. During the meal, I meant to say to her, "Mom, please pass the butter," but instead I said, "Mom, you bitch, you wrecked my entire life."

Rarely is there such a dynamic example of Freudian repression.

At dinner, in the office, or in the bedroom, there comes a point in everyone's life when a cigar is not just a cigar. A point when everyone needs a little help. Simple day-to-day decisions can become overwhelming. Sexual urges, formerly under control, now seem to be controlling you.

Things you once were sure of now keep you up at night. When your libido keeps you from doing your very best, it is time to head to a couch for long, expensive Freudian psychoanalysis.

In this day and age with time short, money short, and all the really good therapists on daytime talk shows, what is the average neurotic person to do? Until now they were up the Danube without a prognosis. Now, however, *Shrink Yourself: The Complete Do-It-Yourself Guide to Freudian Psychoanalysis* allows you, the patient, to have years of in-depth Freudian psychoanalysis for one low price. Never again will you obsess about your next appointment, only to find your self-centered analyst canceling because of some unnecessary family funeral in a far-off state. No more free-floating anxiety about penises, castration, or death swirling around in your head until others have time for you and your paralyzing little problems. Your conscious and unconscious can rest, you can lower those ego defenses and get some well-deserved sleep. That self-destructive and aggressive behavior can be repressed back to the Stone Age. Best of all, you, the patient, get no bill.

Shrink Yourself: The Complete Do-It-Yourself Guide to Freudian Psychoanalysis covers repression, dream analysis, childhood trauma, Freudian slips, neurotic symptoms, sexual repression, Oedipus complex, ink blots, and everyone's favorite—penis envy.

If it affects you, if it is really driving you nuts, *Shrink Yourself: The Complete Do-It-Yourself Guide to Freudian Psychoanalysis* can help you.

HOW TO USE THIS BOOK

hrink Yourself: The Complete Do-It-Yourself Guide to Freudian Psycho-analysis is easy to use. First, find a comfortable couch. Then, starting on page three, respond to all questions asked and follow all directions given. *Shrink Yourself: The Complete Do-It-Yourself Guide to Freudian Psychoanalysis* will guide you through an emotionally-fulfilling Freudian therapy session. Top-notch, $150-per-hour Freudian analytical insight has been inserted at exactly those critical points when a real analyst would have responded. The length of your session is fifty minutes. The topics discussed are up to you.

The direction your session takes is totally up to you. *Shrink Yourself: The Complete Do-It-Yourself Guide to Freudian Psychoanalysis* puts you in control of your therapy session and, as a result, back in control of your life.

Though much of what Freud believed has been disproved in the past few years, one can still compile a lengthy list of highly overpaid analysts who would bet their Beamer, as well as the house payment, on its reliability. All that aside, with the help of *Shrink Yourself: The Complete Do-It-Yourself Guide to Freudian Psychoanalysis,* nothing stands between you and a lifetime of mental well-being, future happiness, and every other darned thing you want and deserve out of life.

THE SESSION BEGINS

First Mr./Ms. _____ (*fill in your name here for a closer doctor–patient relationship*), please lie down on the couch and make yourself comfortable.

I should tell you that I work with a fifty-minute hour.

That means our session is only fifty minutes but you pay for the full hour.

No, Mr./Ms. _____, I am not
trying to cheat you. A fifty-minute hour
is standard.

Now, why don't you start by telling me a bit
about why you are here.

Yes.

Yes.

Yes, go on.

Yes.

Hmmm.

Continue!

Mmmmmmmm . . . Mmm.

MMMMMMM. Ohhhh.

MMMM.

What about your mother?

How do you feel about that?

I think we should take a look at that little
Freudian slip you just made. Why do you think
you said "inquisitor" instead of castrator,
I'm sorry . . . I meant to say mother?

My job is not to tell you what it means,
Mr./Ms. _____.
I am here to help you tell yourself what it means.

NOW CONTINUE!

Yes.

Yes.

Your childhood, yes.

Yes.

Mmmm, go on.

Very interesting.

That is very interesting.

(Cough)

How old were you at this point?

Your mother was there?

How do you feel about that?

This might be a good time to take a break and try some word associations. I will say a word, and you say the first thing that comes to your mind.

Penis.

Mother.

Castration.

Father.

Screwdriver.

Penis.

Doughnut.

Éclair.

Roto-Rooter.

Penis.

Lorena Bobbitt.

Nutcracker.

Banana.

Breasts.

Hot dog.

Clams.

Weed whacker.

Penis.

Sausage.

Cream sauce.

Did you see a pattern in your answers?

Maybe we should analyze this pattern?

Yes.

Yes . . .

Yes.

How does that make you feel?

Interesting.

Yes . . .

MMmmmm.

No.

Yes.

Yes.

Yes.

No.

No.

No.

No.

What?

Let me reassure you that I am not checking my watch because of boredom.

TELL ME ABOUT YOUR DREAMS, PLEASE.

Why do you think you don't remember them?

Everybody dreams.

Well, Mr./Ms. _____,
dreams can be divided into three categories:
first, intelligible; next is bewildering; and the
third—disconnected, confused, and meaningless.

Even if you do not think you do,
Mr./Ms. _____, I can tell you
that you do indeed dream.

Take a moment, maybe you'll think of something.

No? Think harder.

Okay, close your eyes and concentrate.

That's a start.

Yes, a sandwich might mean you're hungry.

Yes, I would be bewildered if I dreamed I was being chased by a sandwich.

By the way, what kind of sandwich was it?

Pastrami on white bread?!

This is turning out to be a much more
complicated and confusing dream.
Can you recall any condiments?

Parsley is not a condiment. It's a garnish.

Was ein kohlkopf.
Oh nothing.

Yes.

Yes.

Yes.

Yes.

Don't get hysterical, Mr./Ms. _____.

The common element in your dream is obvious—it is simple and undisguised wish fulfillment.

Once again, yes, perhaps you were hungry. But let's explore this further.

Yes.

Yes.

Yes.

Pastrami.

Very insightful.

AACHoooo. Excuse me.

Continue, please.

Interesting.

Very interesting.

How often have you dreamt that?

What do you think it means?

What else do you remember?

That's not a garnish. That's a condiment.

Your mother! Was she there too?

Do you think it is important that she was there?

Why don't you tell me.

I don't know what it would mean.

What do you think it might mean?

It might, but then again it might not.
Why don't you tell me.

oh . . . oh . . . OH!

Now tell me more about your mother.

Typical.

It might.

Yes . . .

Yes . . .

Yes.

Yes.

Yes.

Yes.

Yes . . .

No.

It might. What do you think?

How do you feel about that?

That's normal. Go on.

That is not normal.

We seem to be at a slow point here.
Maybe we should change direction a little.
I would now like to try a projective test with you.
It is called the Rorschach ink blot test.

I shall show you a series of ink blots,
and you tell me what you see.
There are no right or wrong answers.
Let us proceed.

Where do you see that?

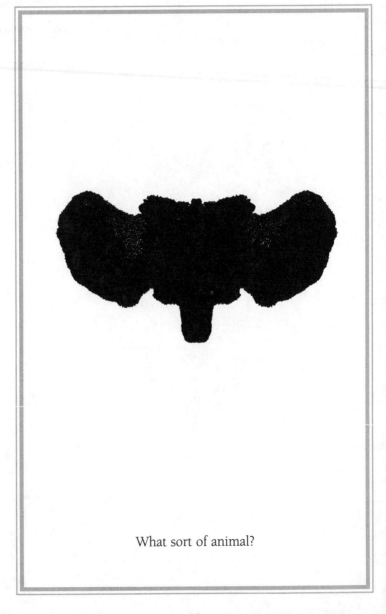

What sort of animal?

You see a what?

There is no wrong direction for an ink blot.
Why, what do you see?

Don't be embarrassed.
Feel free to say anything you want.
Remember, there are no wrong answers.

Now let's try to put it all together.

What did you notice about all your answers today?

Yes.

Well, yes.

Well, yes . . . but . . .

But about the similarities in your answers . . .

What about your mother?

I don't know, I wasn't there. You tell me.

Yes . . .

Yes.
No.
Yes.

You know that answer if you would just think about it.

No, I am not bored, and I am not going to tell you again.

I hate to say it, but we are just about out of time.
I think we made some progress today.
What do you think?

I'm sorry but I have to go.
I have another patient waiting.

I am going to give you a few prescriptions that I think will help calm you down. Please be sure to get them filled immediately. You may refill them as often as you need.

Remember to fill in your name and address on these personalized prescription forms. Remember to take drugs only as prescribed, and never overmedicate yourself.

SIGMUND FREUD M.D.
VIENNA, AUSTRIA

NAME_____ DATE_____
ADDRESS_____

R

Darvon

REFILL ____ TIMES   _____M.D.
NO. REFILLS ____   LIC .0000098 4354677

SIGMUND FREUD M.D.
VIENNA, AUSTRIA

NAME_____ DATE_____
ADDRESS_____

R

Halcion

REFILL ____ TIMES   _____M.D.
NO. REFILLS ____   LIC .0000098 4354677

If those medications don't work, please try these
and remember to never overmedicate yourself.

SIGMUND FREUD M.D.
VIENNA, AUSTRIA

NAME_____ DATE_____

ADDRESS_____

R

Lithium

REFILL ____ TIMES   _____M.D.

NO. REFILLS ____   LIC .0000098 4354677

SIGMUND FREUD M.D.
VIENNA, AUSTRIA

NAME_____ DATE_____

ADDRESS_____

R

Prozac

REFILL ____ TIMES   _____M.D.

NO. REFILLS ____   LIC .0000098 4354677

Medication is a very inexact science. In case those other drugs don't work, please try these and remember to never overmedicate yourself.

✂ -

SIGMUND FREUD M.D.
VIENNA, AUSTRIA

NAME_____ DATE_____
ADDRESS_____

℞

valium

REFILL ____ TIMES   _____M.D.
NO. REFILLS ____   LIC .0000098 4354677

- -

SIGMUND FREUD M.D.
VIENNA, AUSTRIA

NAME_____ DATE_____
ADDRESS_____

℞

Paxil

REFILL ____ TIMES   _____M.D.
NO. REFILLS ____   LIC .0000098 4354677

Oh, before you go, Mr./Ms. _____,
here's a little handout of symbols that seem
to recur in many of my patients' dreams.
Understand that not all symbols mean the same
thing every time, and, in fact, they probably
mean something different for every person.
Sometimes they are meaningless and take up
valuable brain cells better used for other very
important stuff. But in spite of that, I think you
should study these closely—maybe they'll help
you interpret your dreams until you return for
your next session.

I'm also giving you a diary to keep track of your
dream imagery, which will help you to interpret
your own dreams.

Please be sure you have paid the receptionist on your way out. I will see you at your next appointment.

No. I don't accept insurance.

Auf Wiedersehen.

COMMON DREAM SYMBOLS

<u>SYMBOL</u>

<u>POSSIBLE MEANING</u>

Train entering tunnel   Sex

Volcanic eruption   Sex

Entering a room   Sex

Leaving a room   Leaving after sex

Rocket launch   Sex

SYMBOL	POSSIBLE MEANING
Eating chocolate	Sex
Playing the accordion	Kinky sex
Banana	Penis
Doughnut	Who cares?
Jackhammer	Sex
Having sex	You're dreaming
Reading a book	Broken TV
Sausage	Breakfast
Dogs playing poker	Sex
Monkey wearing fez	Anxiety
Wanting a Corvette	Wanting a larger penis
Vacuuming	Sex

SYMBOL	POSSIBLE MEANING
Watching TV	Lack of sex
Surfing the Internet	Desperate lack of sex
Changing a light bulb	Sex
Drinking water	Thirsty
Washing dishes	Dirty dishes
Grocery shopping	Buy sausages
Sleeping	Tired
Old Faithful	Sex
Geometry	Failure
Trigonometry	Total failure
Garden hose	Sex
Cigar	Sometimes is just a cigar

Use these forms to keep track of your dreams.

Remember, displacement and pictorial arrangement, leading to preliminary interpretation, supported by secondary interpolation, in combination with psychical material will help you evaluate your dreams. However, the erection of a dream façade may or may not frequently represent a transformation of wishful fantasies. Also keep in mind that manifest or latent content may or may not coincide with your conclusions.

And remember, this should be fun.

My Personal Dream Diary

Date _____

My dream_____

_____

_____

_____

Dream symbols _____

_____

_____

What I think it means _____

_____

_____

Do I need help? ❑ Yes ❑ No ❑ Maybe

My Personal Dream Diary

Date _____

My dream_____

_____

_____

_____

Dream symbols _____

_____

_____

What I think it means _____

_____

_____

Do I need help? ☐ Yes ☐ No ☐ Maybe

My Personal Dream Diary

Date _____

My dream _____

_____

_____

_____

Dream symbols _____

_____

_____

What I think it means _____

_____

_____

Do I need help? ❑ Yes ❑ No ❑ Maybe

My Personal Dream Diary

Date _____

My dream_____

_____

_____

_____

Dream symbols _____

_____

_____

What I think it means _____

_____

_____

Do I need help? ❏ Yes ❏ No ❏ Maybe

My Personal Dream Diary

Date _____

My dream_____

_____

_____

_____

Dream symbols _____

_____

_____

What I think it means _____

_____

_____

Do I need help? ❑ Yes ❑ No ❑ Maybe